THE SECRET
Gratitude Book

RHONDA
BYRNE

Introduction

Whenever I am asked the easiest way to use *The Secret,* my answer is always the same. Gratitude! It is one of the most powerful emotions you can use to bring all-good into your life in absolute abundance. No matter who you are, no matter where you are, gratitude can dissolve all negativity in your life, no matter what form it has taken. Let me explain how something as simple as gratitude can completely transform your life.

The Secret explains that the law of attraction is the most powerful law in the Universe. This magnificent law governs all energy, attracting like energy to like energy. Einstein proved that *everything* in the Universe is energy. All energy vibrates at particular frequencies. We are energy too, and so each of us is also vibrating at a frequency. Your thoughts, feelings, and beliefs determine the vibration and frequency of your energy.

As you focus on gratitude and think, speak, and feel gratitude, you are transforming your energy frequency into one of the most powerful and highest frequencies of all. Gratitude attracts like energy of gratitude to it, so as you are feeling grateful you are powerfully bringing like energies to you, which will have you experience more things to be grateful for. In other words, you will magnetize to you the energy of people, circumstances, and events that will bring all good into your life.

It is impossible to bring more good into your life if you are feeling ungrateful for what you have. Why? Because the thoughts and feelings you emit as you feel ungrateful attract a life filled with more things to feel ungrateful about. Whether it is jealousy, resentment, dissatisfaction, or feelings of "not enough," those negative emotions cannot bring you what you want. They are blocking your own good coming to you. If you want a new car but you are not grateful for the car you have, that will be the dominant frequency you are sending out, and you cannot attract something better. On the other hand, if you feel grateful for the car you have now, you are powerfully summoning an even better car to you.

The negative things that we experience in life are simply caused by turning away from all the good that is there. Imagine that the Universe (which is all-good) is like the sun. The sun continually shines, sending out its life energy to us in a never-ending stream. You experience the effect of the sun when you are facing it, but if you turn away you will no longer receive its live-giving effects.

The Universe is operating identically to the sun. It is always there and always available, sending out all-good to you. When you focus your thoughts and feelings on gratitude you are turning toward all the good that is being permanently offered to you. But when you complain, blame, criticize, feel resentment, jealousy, or any negative emotion, you are turning away from all that is good.

The Secret Gratitude Book is one of the most powerful tools you can ever use to transform your life into total joy. When you use the book every day and write about all the things in your life you are grateful for, you will be amazed at the never-ending list of thoughts that come back to you of more things to be grateful for. You just have to make a start, and then the law of attraction will receive those grateful thoughts and give you more just like them. To transform your life, you must find a way of being grateful for what you have now. As you focus on sincere gratitude for several minutes at a time, you will move your frequency to one of the most powerful frequencies there is, and all-good things will begin to appear in your life!

You can also use gratitude and *The Secret Gratitude Book* to powerfully attract specific things that you want into your life. When you are grateful for the things that you *want* to come into your life (the perfect relationship, the dream job, absolute health, total abundance) *before* they actually appear, you are sending out a frequency to the Universe that you *already have those things*. The law of attraction does not know if you are imagining something or if it is real, so by giving heartfelt thanks for it *now*, you must attract those things to you. This is an immutable law, and when used correctly it is unfailing in its response.

The Secret Gratitude Book is filled with pieces
I have written that can bring joy and harmony
to every aspect of your life. To maximize all the
power of these words of wisdom and truth, read
them slowly, say each word emphatically and
with intensity, and feel them deeply within your
heart.

1   Before you begin to write anything, sit
     quietly and silently say "Thank you" twenty
     times. Feel the feelings of gratitude as you
     silently repeat the words "Thank you."

2   Always list the things you are grateful for in
     the present tense, whether you have them
     now or not. If you write the things you want
     as being in the future, then they will always
     be in the future. For example, "I am so
     grateful for all the abundance that will
     come to me" could result in the abundance
     always just "coming" . . . and not arriving!
     To harness the power of the law of attraction,

you have to give thanks NOW for the things you want, as though you have already received them.

3   When writing your list, begin each sentence with "I am truly grateful for…" Or "I am so grateful now that…" Or "Thank you for…" Or any other similar words of gratitude that feel good to you.

4   First write down the things you are grateful for in your life now on the page marked "Gratitude Now" and feel the feelings as deeply as possible with your heart.

5   When you have finished your daily "Gratitude Now" list, move to the opposite page marked "Gratitude Intentions" and immediately write down your gratitude list for all the things you want to come into your life. Remember to write them as though you have them now, and begin each sentence in the same way as your "Gratitude Now" list.

Tips TO ADD INCREDIBLE POWER TO
YOUR DAILY GRATITUDE PROCESS

1 As you silently say "Thank you," imagine
that the words are being spoken through
your heart. This is incredibly powerful.

2 You can also decide to use the silent
"Thank you" process in between
your "Gratitude Now" list and your
"Gratitude Intentions" list.

3 In addition, you can use the silent
"Thank you" process, spoken through
your heart, at the end of your daily
gratitude lists as you close your book.

4 Each day make it a habit to feel the feelings
of gratitude in advance for the great day
ahead, as though it is done.

5 As you walk from one place to another,
think and feel the words "Thank you"
in your heart with every step. You will be
thinking something when you walk, so

why not use this time to "milk" the Universe with gratitude? The Universe wants to give you everything you want to live a full life, and it is eternally pressing down all-good to every single person—in every moment of their life.

I cannot even begin to describe the unfathomable power you are summoning through the Universe when you do these things.

The more you use gratitude every day, the greater the good you will bring into your life. It is all you have to do to completely transform your life in every single area, and on every single subject. There are no limits to the good that you can bring forth to you, and by practicing gratitude daily, you will increase and maximize your magnetic power to attract a life beyond your wildest dreams. And for you to live a life beyond your wildest dreams is my dream come true.

Rhonda Byrne, author of *The Secret*

THE SECRET
Gratitude Book

Gratitude Now

_____
_____
_____
_____
_____
_____
_____
_____
_____
_____
_____
_____
_____
_____
_____
_____
_____
_____
_____
_____
_____

THE BEST LIFE HAS TO GIVE
IS MINE NOW. THANK YOU!

Gratitude Intentions

Gratitude Now

Dankie

AS BELOW
AS IS ABOVE
SO WITH

I AM SO GRATEFUL THAT
MY BODY IS CREATING
PERFECT HEALTH AND
HARMONY.

Gratitude Now

THANK YOU FOR THE
ABUNDANCE THAT IS
COMING TO ME EVERY DAY.

Gratitude Intentions

Спасибо

Gratitude Now

Gràcies

Gratitude Intentions

YOU CAN FEEL YOUR HEART
CALLING YOU HOME TO
LOVE AND GRATITUDE.

Gratitude Now

_____

_____

_____

_____

_____

_____

_____

_____

_____

_____

_____

_____

_____

_____

_____

_____

_____

_____

I AM SO DEEPLY GRATEFUL
THAT I AM THE MASTER OF
MY MIND.

Gratitude Intentions

謝謝

Gratitude Now

謝謝

Gratitude Intentions

I AM GRATEFUL THAT ALL
THE WISDOM AND BEAUTY
OF THE UNIVERSE IS BEING
EXPRESSED THROUGH ME.

Gratitude Now

_____

_____

_____

_____

_____

_____

_____

_____

_____

_____

_____

_____

_____

_____

_____

_____

_____

_____

_____

_____

I AM DEEPLY GRATEFUL
THAT PEACE IS APPEARING
IN MY HOME, IN MY HEART,
AND IN ALL MY AFFAIRS.

Gratitude Intentions

Gratitude Now

Děkuji

Gratitude Intentions

SAY AND FEEL "THANK YOU"
THROUGH YOUR HEART,
WITH EVERY STEP YOU TAKE.

Gratitude Now

_____

_____

_____

_____

_____

_____

_____

_____

_____

_____

_____

_____

_____

_____

I AM GRATEFUL THAT
I AM THE BRILLIANT
CONSCIOUS CREATOR OF
MY LIFE AND THEREFORE
ALL THINGS IN MY LIFE
CAN BE CREATED OR
CHANGED THROUGH MY
CONSCIOUS DIRECTION.

Gratitude Intentions

Gratitude Now

Gratitude Intentions

I AM TRULY GRATEFUL
FOR THE NEW PEOPLE,
CIRCUMSTANCES, AND
EVENTS THAT ARE
BRINGING JOY INTO
MY LIFE.

Gratitude Now

_____

_____

_____

_____

_____

_____

_____

_____

_____

_____

_____

_____

_____

_____

_____

_____

_____

_____

_____

_____

I AM GRATEFUL THAT
EVERYTHING IN LIFE
IS COMING TO ME
EFFORTLESSLY AND
EASILY AT ALL TIMES.

Gratitude Intentions

Gratitude Now

THERE IS A POWER WITHIN
ME THAT IS GREATER
THAN THE WORLD. TO
IGNITE THE POWER OF THE
UNIVERSE IN ME, I MUST
BE IN HARMONY WITH
LOVE AND GRATITUDE.

Gratitude Now

I AM TRULY GRATEFUL TO
KNOW THAT SIMPLY BY
USING MY IMAGINATION,
I CAN BRING WHAT I AM
IMAGINING TO ME.

Gratitude Intentions

Merci

Gratitude Now

Danke

Gratitude Intentions

THANK YOU FOR MY
ABILITY TO LOVE, WHICH
KNOWS NO LIMITS.

Gratitude Now

I GIVE THANKS THAT MY
MIND IS ILLUMINATED
WITH UNLIMITED
POSSIBILITIES, AND I CAN
SEE THEM WITH CLARITY
IN ALL SITUATIONS,
WITHOUT ANY EFFORT.

Gratitude Intentions

Gratitude Now

Gratitude Intentions

GIVING HEARTFELT
THANKS CAUSES YOUR
DREAMS TO COME TRUE.

Gratitude Now

_____
_____
_____
_____
_____
_____
_____
_____
_____
_____
_____
_____
_____
_____
_____
_____
_____
_____
_____
_____
_____

THANK YOU FOR THE LOVE
OF THE UNIVERSE THAT
WILL SURROUND ME IN
EVERYTHING I DO TODAY.

Gratitude Intentions

Gratitude Now

Grazie

Gratitude Intentions

I AM CREATING
NEW THOUGHTS,
BETTER THOUGHTS,
GREATER THOUGHTS,
AND SUPERIOR THOUGHTS,
TODAY AND EVERY DAY.
THANK YOU.

Gratitude Now

_____

_____

_____

_____

_____

_____

_____

_____

_____

_____

_____

_____

_____

_____

_____

_____

_____

THANK YOU FOR THE
FUN, LAUGHTER, AND
JOYOUS SURPRISES
THAT WILL FLOOD
INTO MY LIFE TODAY.

Gratitude Intentions

ありがとう　こうがい

Gratitude Now

THE POWER OF LOVE AND
GRATITUDE WILL DISSOLVE
ALL NEGATIVITY IN OUR
LIVES, NO MATTER WHAT
FORM IT HAS TAKEN.

Gratitude Now

_____

_____

_____

_____

_____

_____

_____

_____

_____

_____

_____

_____

_____

_____

_____

_____

_____

I GIVE THANKS THAT MY
CELLS ARE ATTRACTING
ABSOLUTE WELL-BEING
AND COMPLETE HARMONY
IN MY BODY NOW.

Gratitude Intentions

Gratitude Now

_____

_____

_____

_____

_____

_____

_____

_____

_____

_____

_____

_____

_____

_____

_____

_____

_____

_____

_____

_____

_____

_____

TODAY I AM FEELING LOVE
AND IMMENSE GRATITUDE
FOR THOSE PEOPLE WHO
ARE CHALLENGING ME IN
MY LIFE. AND I KNOW MY
LOVE AND GRATITUDE WILL
DISSOLVE ALL NEGATIVITY.

Gratitude Now

I GIVE THANKS THAT ALL
MY NEEDS ARE MET IN
EVERY SINGLE MOMENT.

Gratitude Intentions

Obrigado

AS ABOVE

Gratitude Now

Gratitude Intentions

APPRECIATE AND BE
GRATEFUL FOR EVERY
LITTLE THING!

Gratitude Now

_____

_____

_____

_____

_____

_____

_____

_____

_____

_____

_____

_____

_____

_____

_____

_____

_____

THANK YOU FOR ALL THE
GOOD THAT IS BEING
EXPRESSED IN EVERY AREA
OF MY LIFE.

Gratitude Intentions

Спасибо

Gratitude Now

Gratitude Intentions

I GIVE THANKS FOR THE
JOY AND LOVE THAT
SURROUNDS MY ENTIRE
FAMILY AND ALL MY
FRIENDS.

Gratitude Now

TODAY I AM LETTING GO
OF ALL NEGATIVE FEELINGS
ABOUT ME. BLAME, BE
GONE. UNWORTHINESS,
BE GONE. DOUBT, BE GONE.
GUILT, BE GONE.

Gratitude Intentions

I WELCOME ALL MY GOOD
THOUGHTS ABOUT ME.
I COMMAND THEM TO ME.
I EMBRACE THEM. I GIVE
THE DEEPEST THANKS
FOR THEM.

Gratitude Now

Gratitude Intentions

YOU CAN CHANGE
ANYTHING AND
EVERYTHING WITH
GRATITUDE.

Gratitude Now

I AM SO GRATEFUL THAT
I AM NOW CREATING A
LIFE BEYOND MY WILDEST
DREAMS.

Gratitude Intentions

Gracias

AS ABOVE

Gratitude Now

Tack

I AM TRULY GRATEFUL
TO KNOW THAT I AM
THE CREATOR OF MY LIFE,
AND THAT I HAVE THE
POWER TO DO ANYTHING.

Gratitude Now

_____

_____

_____

_____

_____

_____

_____

_____

_____

_____

_____

_____

_____

_____

_____

_____

_____

THANK YOU FOR THE
GIFT OF MY LIFE TODAY.
TODAY IS THE BEST DAY
OF MY LIFE.

Gratitude Intentions

Gratitude Now

Thank you

Gratitude Intentions

JUST BEING ALIVE IS
ENOUGH TO INSPIRE
A CONSTANT RUSH OF
GRATITUDE.

Gratitude Now

_____

_____

_____

_____

_____

_____

_____

_____

_____

_____

_____

_____

_____

_____

_____

_____

_____

TODAY, AS I MOVE
THROUGH MY DAY, I WILL
SEE THE BEAUTY THAT
SURROUNDS ME, AND
I WILL GIVE THANKS FOR
IT ALL.

Gratitude Intentions

Gratitude Now

благодаря

Gratitude Intentions

I AM SO GRATEFUL TO
KNOW THAT AS I FOCUS
ON A PERSON AND FEEL
THE FEELINGS OF LOVE FOR
THEM IN MY HEART... THE
LOVE WILL REACH THEM.

Gratitude Now

_____

_____

_____

_____

_____

_____

_____

_____

_____

_____

_____

_____

_____

_____

_____

_____

_____

_____

I AM THE JOY AND THE
LOVE OF THE UNIVERSE.
THANK YOU FOR THE JOY
OF BEING ME.

Gratitude Intentions

Gracias

Gratitude Now

謝謝
謝謝

Gratitude Intentions

LOVE AND GRATITUDE CAN
PART SEAS, THEY CAN MOVE
MOUNTAINS, AND THEY
CAN CREATE MIRACLES.

Gratitude Now

_____

_____

_____

_____

_____

_____

_____

_____

_____

_____

_____

_____

_____

_____

_____

_____

_____

_____

_____

I AM DEEPLY GRATEFUL FOR
THE MAGIC AND MIRACLES
THAT WILL FOLLOW ME
EVERYWHERE I GO TODAY.

Gratitude Intentions

謝謝

AS ABOVE

Gratitude Now

Gratitude Intentions

THANK YOU FOR THE
GREAT NEWS THAT IS
COMING TO ME TODAY.

Gratitude Now

WITH THE DEEPEST
GRATITUDE AND FAITH,
I KNOW THAT EVERYTHING
IS HAPPENING PERFECTLY
FOR ME.

Gratitude Intentions

Gratitude Now

Gratitude Intentions

WOULDN'T NOW BE
A REALLY GOOD TIME
TO BE GRATEFUL FOR
TOMORROW? THIS ONE
ACT WILL TRANSFORM
YOUR TOMORROW
INTO JOY.

Gratitude Now

THANK YOU FOR THE
LOVE THAT I FEEL RADIATE
FROM ME WHEN I FOCUS
INTENSELY ON THE
FEELINGS IN MY HEART.

Gratitude Intentions

Gratitude Now

Gratitude Intentions

I AM SO GRATEFUL
THAT I AM UNLIMITED,
AND THAT I CAN DO,
BE, OR HAVE ANYTHING
MY HEART DESIRES.

Gratitude Now

I GIVE THANKS FOR THE
GIFT OF TODAY.

Gratitude Intentions

Gratitude Now

Merci

Gratitude Intentions

WITH EVERY CHECK
YOU WRITE, FEEL DEEP
GRATITUDE FOR WHAT
WAS GIVEN TO YOU.

Gratitude Now

_____
_____
_____
_____
_____
_____
_____
_____
_____
_____
_____
_____
_____
_____
_____
_____
_____
_____
_____
_____
_____
_____

I AM SO GRATEFUL THAT
THE UNIVERSE WILL THRILL
ME WITH MAGNIFICENT
SURPRISES TODAY.

Gratitude Intentions

Gratitude Now

Gratitude Intentions

I GIVE THANKS
THAT MY HEART IS
OVERFLOWING WITH
PEACE, LOVE, AND JOY.

Gratitude Now

THANK YOU FOR ALL
THE WONDERS THAT
POUR INTO MY LIFE.

Gratitude Intentions

Gratitude Now

Terima kasih

Gratitude Intentions

THE MOST POWERFUL
PRAYER IS ONE OF THANKS.

Gratitude Now

I AM GRATEFUL FOR THE
HARMONY AND PEACE
THAT REIGN SUPREME
IN MY MIND.

Gratitude Intentions

Gratitude Now

あ り が と う

Gratitude Intentions

I AM SO GRATEFUL FOR
THE LOVE AND JOY THAT
SURROUNDS ME TODAY.

Gratitude Now

I KNOW THAT A THANKFUL
HEART IS ALWAYS CLOSE TO
THE CREATIVE ENERGIES OF
THE UNIVERSE.

Gratitude Intentions

Gratitude Now

Takk

Gratitude Intentions

THANK YOUR WAY
TO HEALTH, WEALTH,
AND HAPPINESS!

Gratitude Now

I GIVE THANKS THAT I AM
BECOMING MORE AND
MORE AWARE EVERY DAY.

Gratitude Intentions

Gratitude Now

Obrigado

I GIVE THANKS THAT I AM
ETERNALLY YOUNG, AND
THAT MY BODY IS BEING
PERPETUALLY RENEWED.

Gratitude Now

I GIVE THANKS THAT
THE PERFECT, THE GREAT,
AND THE BEAUTIFUL ARE
EXPRESSING THEMSELVES
THROUGH ME.

Gratitude Intentions

Gratitude Now

Gratitude Intentions

FEEL LOVE AND GRATITUDE
FOR EVERYONE AND
EVERYTHING... EVERY DAY.

Gratitude Now

_____

_____

_____

_____

_____

_____

_____

_____

_____

_____

_____

_____

_____

_____

_____

_____

_____

_____

_____

I GIVE THANKS THAT I AM
SUPREME WISDOM, LOVE,
AND POWER.

Gratitude Intentions

Gratitude Now

Ďakujem vám

Gratitude Intentions

I WILL SEE AND
EXPERIENCE ABUNDANCE
SURROUNDING ME TODAY.
THANK YOU.

Gratitude Now

I AM THE PERFECTION
OF LIFE. THANK YOU.

Gratitude Intentions

Gratitude Now

Gracias

Gratitude Intentions

WHAT ARE YOU GRATEFUL
FOR RIGHT NOW?

Gratitude Now

_____

_____

_____

_____

_____

_____

_____

_____

_____

_____

_____

_____

_____

_____

_____

_____

_____

_____

I AM SO GRATEFUL THAT
MY TRUST AND FAITH
IN THE UNIVERSE ARE
INCREASING EVERY DAY.

Gratitude Intentions

Gratitude Now

Teşekkür ederim

Gratitude Intentions

WITH GRATITUDE I ASK.
THROUGH GRATITUDE
I BELIEVE. AND IN
GRATITUDE I RECEIVE
WHATEVER MY HEART
DESIRES.

Gratitude Now

THANK YOU. I AM AN
UNLIMITED BEING AND
I HAVE ALL KNOWLEDGE,
WISDOM, LOVE, AND
POWER, NOW.

Gratitude Intentions

Thank you

Gratitude Now

Dankie

Gratitude Intentions

THE TRUE BEAUTY OF LIFE
IS REVEALED WHEN YOU
HAVE A GRATEFUL HEART.

Gratitude Now

I AM TRULY GRATEFUL
THAT I HAVE AN
ABUNDANCE OF TIME
EVERY SINGLE DAY.

Gratitude Intentions

благодаря

Gratitude Now

Gràcies

Gratitude Intentions

I AM SO GRATEFUL TO
BE ALIVE.

Gratitude Now

_____

_____

_____

_____

_____

_____

_____

_____

_____

_____

_____

_____

_____

_____

_____

_____

_____

_____

_____

_____

_____

I AM SO GRATEFUL FOR THE
CONTINUOUS WELL-BEING
THAT IS MANIFESTING IN
MY BODY.

Gratitude Intentions

Gratitude Now

Gratitude Intentions

AS YOU FALL ASLEEP AT
NIGHT TAKE A MINUTE TO
THINK BACK OVER THE DAY.
REMEMBER THE MOMENTS
THAT WERE WONDERFUL,
AND GIVE THANKS FOR
EACH ONE OF THEM.

Gratitude Now

_____
_____
_____
_____
_____
_____
_____
_____
_____
_____
_____
_____
_____
_____
_____
_____
_____
_____
_____

I AM SO GRATEFUL THAT I
AM SEEING THE TRUTH OF
LIFE WITH MORE CLARITY
EVERY DAY.

Gratitude Intentions

Gratitude Now

Děkuji

Gratitude Intentions

I GIVE THANKS
THAT MY HEART AND
MY INTUITION ARE
GUIDING ME EVERY DAY.

Gratitude Now

_____

_____

_____

_____

_____

_____

_____

_____

_____

_____

_____

_____

_____

_____

_____

_____

_____

THANK YOU FOR MY
STRONG CHARACTER
AND MY BRILLIANT MIND.

Gratitude Intentions

Gratitude Now

Dank u

Gratitude Intentions

TEARS OF GRATITUDE
COME FROM A HEART
THAT IS COMPLETELY
CONNECTED WITH THE
LOVE OF THE UNIVERSE.

Gratitude Now

_____
_____
_____
_____
_____
_____
_____
_____
_____
_____
_____
_____
_____
_____
_____
_____
_____
_____
_____

I GIVE THANKS THAT
I AM THINKING NEW
THOUGHTS AND SUPERIOR
THOUGHTS ON ALL
SUBJECTS AT ALL TIMES.

Gratitude Intentions

Gratitude Now

I AM GRATEFUL THAT
SIMPLY BY LIVING MY LIFE,
I AM EXPANDING AND
GROWING EVERY DAY.

Gratitude Now

MY MIND IS IN PERFECT
CONSCIOUS TOUCH WITH
THE INTELLIGENCE OF THE
UNIVERSE. THANK YOU.
THANK YOU. THANK YOU.

Gratitude Intentions

Gratitude Now

Danke

Gratitude Intentions

A GRATEFUL PERSON
IS THANKFUL UNDER
ALL CIRCUMSTANCES.

Gratitude Now

I GIVE THANKS AS I LET GO
OF THE OLD AND ALLOW
THE NEW TO POUR INTO
MY LIFE.

Gratitude Intentions

Gratitude Now

Takk fyrir

Gratitude Intentions

I AM GETTING BETTER
AND BETTER EVERY DAY
IN EVERY WAY. THANK YOU.

Gratitude Now

_____

_____

_____

_____

_____

_____

_____

_____

_____

_____

_____

_____

_____

_____

_____

_____

_____

I GIVE THANKS THAT
I AM CREATING ALL IN
THIS LIFE. THERE IS AN
ABUNDANCE OF TIME
AND I HAVE ALL THE TIME
I NEED TO CREATE ALL.

Gratitude Intentions

Gratitude Now

Grazie

Gratitude Intentions

THERE IS NOT A SINGLE
THING IN LIFE MORE
IMPORTANT THAN
GIVING THANKS.

Gratitude Now

I GIVE THANKS THAT
MY MIND IS RENEWED
IN EVERY MOMENT.

Gratitude Intentions

あ
り
が
と
う

Gratitude Now

Gratitude Intentions

I GIVE THANKS THAT THE
UNIVERSE IS SUPPORTING
ME IN EVERY SINGLE
THING I DO, EVERY DAY.

Gratitude Now

_____

_____

_____

_____

_____

_____

_____

_____

_____

_____

_____

_____

_____

_____

_____

_____

_____

_____

_____

I AM SO GRATEFUL THAT
THE LAW OF ATTRACTION
IS MY BEST FRIEND.

Gratitude Intentions

Gratitude Now

Dziękuję

Gratitude Intentions

YOU CAN CHANGE
ANYTHING, AND THE
PATH IS GRATITUDE.

Gratitude Now

I CAN BREATHE! I AM
ALIVE! HOW BEAUTIFUL.
THANK YOU.

Gratitude Intentions

Gratitude Now

Mulțumesc

Gratitude Intentions

THERE IS NO ONE ELSE
I WANT TO BE. I AM SO
GRATEFUL TO BE ME.

Gratitude Now

_____

_____

_____

_____

_____

_____

_____

_____

_____

_____

_____

_____

_____

_____

_____

_____

_____

_____

_____

THANK YOU FOR MY
MAGNIFICENT LIFE.

Gratitude Intentions